The Baby Chicks

Julia Metzler

Copyright © 2022 Julia Metzler

All rights reserved. No part of this publication may be reproduced, distributed, or transmitted in any form or by any means, including photocopying, recording, or other electronic or mechanical methods, without the prior written permission of the publisher, except in the case of brief quotations embodied in critical reviews and certain other noncommercial uses permitted by copyright law.

For permission requests, write to the publisher through Aurora Borealis Publishing's website.

Paperback ISBN: 978-1-7781373-2-7

Any references to historical events, real people, or real places are used fictitiously. Names, characters, and places are products of the author's imagination.

Cover images by Julia Metzler

Second edition 2022

Aurora Borealis Publishing

www.auroraborealispub.wixsite.com/website

Dedicated to my four baby chicks,

Kalea, Jayce, Laila and Nash

who make everyday a wonderful adventure

It was a snowy and cold February afternoon, and Mom had picked us up from school. She told us, "Get in the car. We are going on an adventure!"

We drove down the hill from school
and headed onto the highway.
"Where are we going?" we asked.
"You'll see..." Mom said with a smile.

We turned off the highway and drove some more. Soon we saw a sign that said Fort McMurray 468 First Nation. We saw dogs sitting in the middle of the road, and they started to follow us! We laughed and waved at them through the window.

Mom stopped at a house at the end of the road. A sign on a tree said "FRESH EGGS $5".

A lady came out the front door of the house with a carton of colorful eggs! She handed them to Mom and said, "I hope these eggs hatch for you! They are a wonderful mix of eggs!"

We all squealed in delight and chattered happily the rest of the drive home. We made plans for the new babies we would be bringing home.

When we got home, Mom pulled out a box with a plastic container inside. "This is an incubator," Mom said. "It will keep the eggs warm like a Mama hen would." She carefully put the eggs into the incubator, added a little bit of water to the bottom of the container and closed the lid.

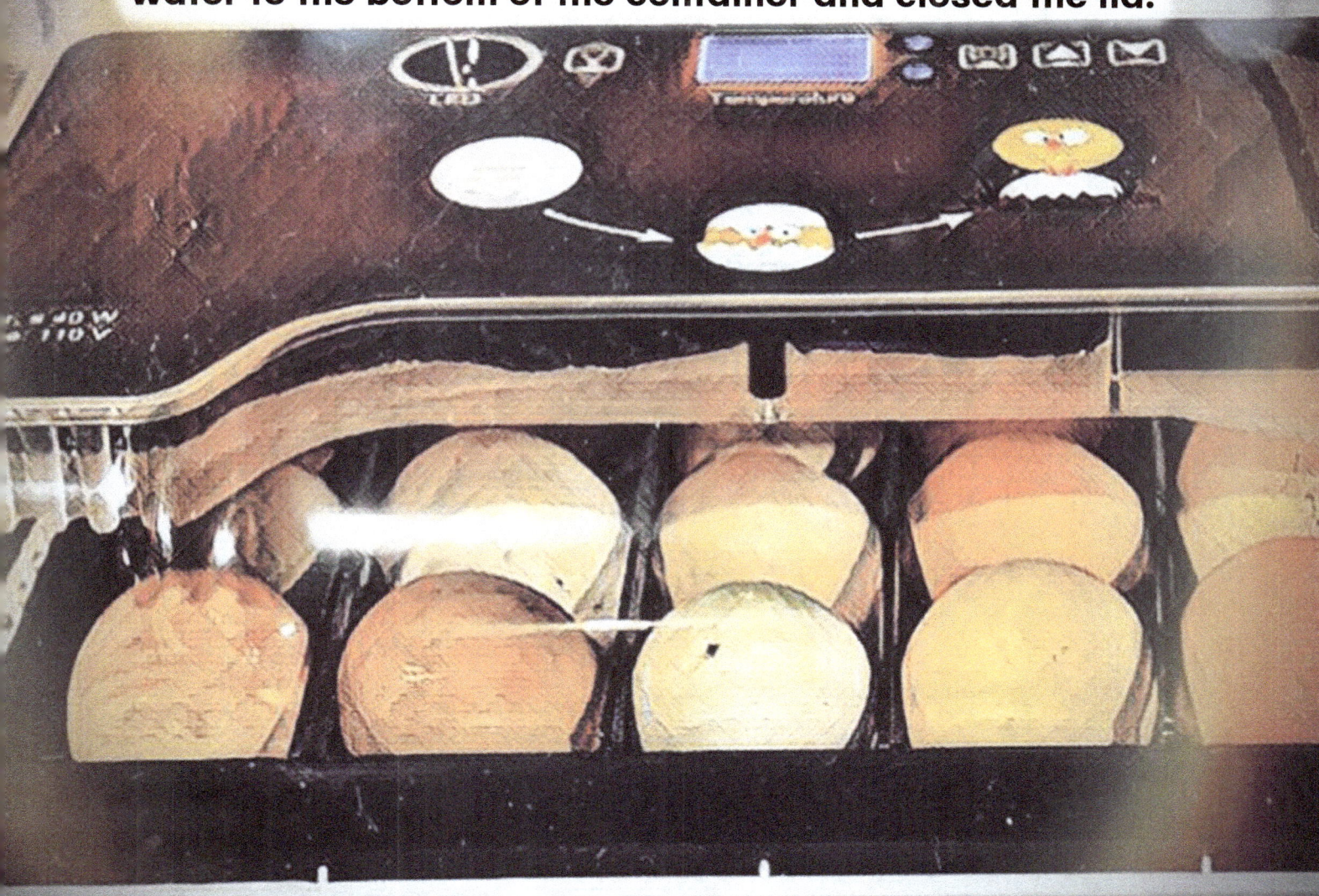

"When will they hatch?" we asked, excitedly. "In twenty-one days." said Mom. We jumped for joy and began our chicken hatching journey!

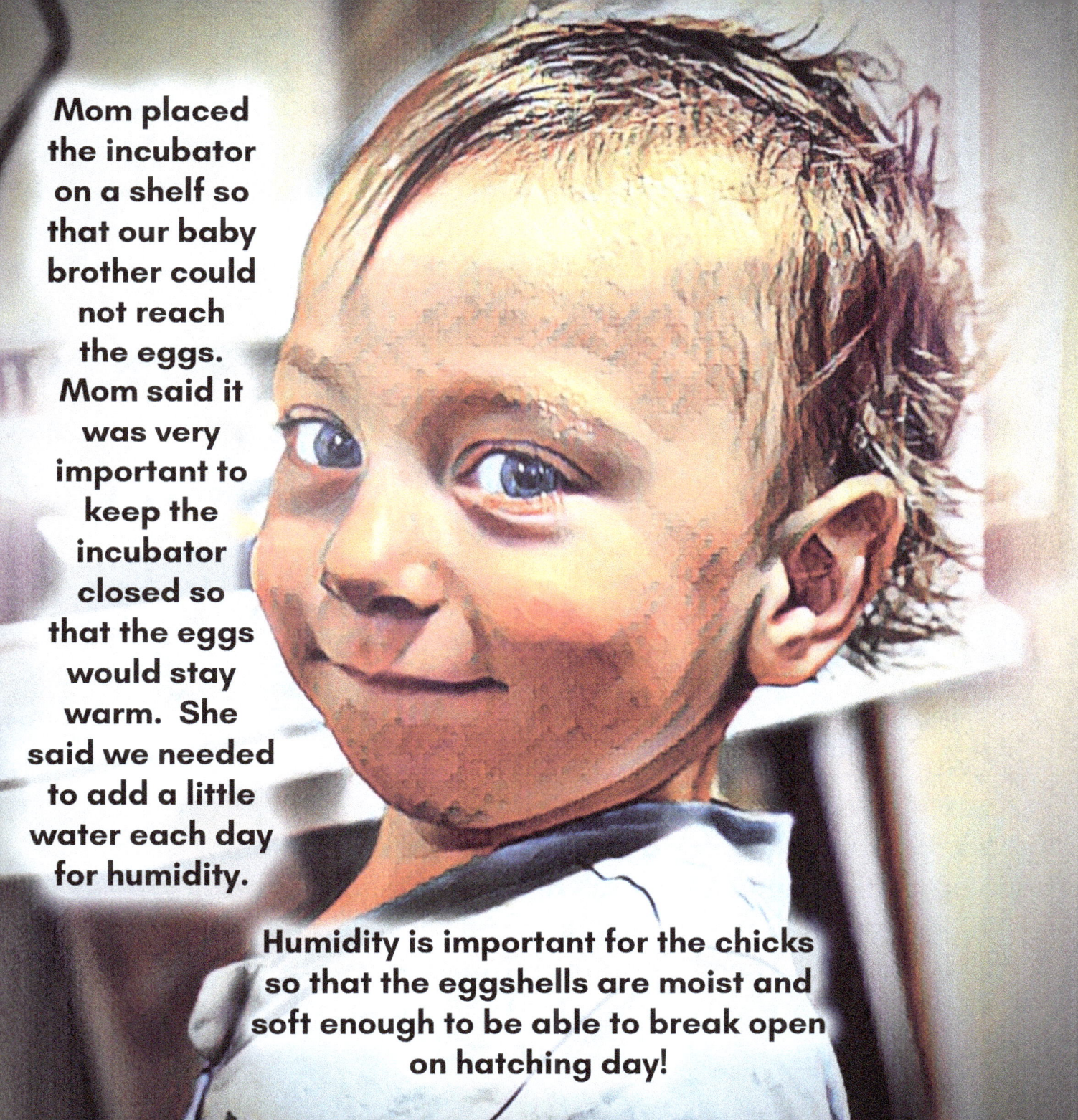

Mom placed the incubator on a shelf so that our baby brother could not reach the eggs. Mom said it was very important to keep the incubator closed so that the eggs would stay warm. She said we needed to add a little water each day for humidity.

Humidity is important for the chicks so that the eggshells are moist and soft enough to be able to break open on hatching day!

We waited and waited and waited some more! Mom would let us take the eggs out of the incubator to candle them. Candling is when you put a bright light under the egg to see how the embryo, baby chick, is growing.

Mom said that some of the eggs might not be fertilized by a daddy rooster so the baby will not grow. These eggs are called "yolkers" and are the kind of eggs we eat for breakfast! She said some of the fertilized eggs might just stop developing too. Those eggs are called "quitters". The eggs that grow and hatch are the "winners"!

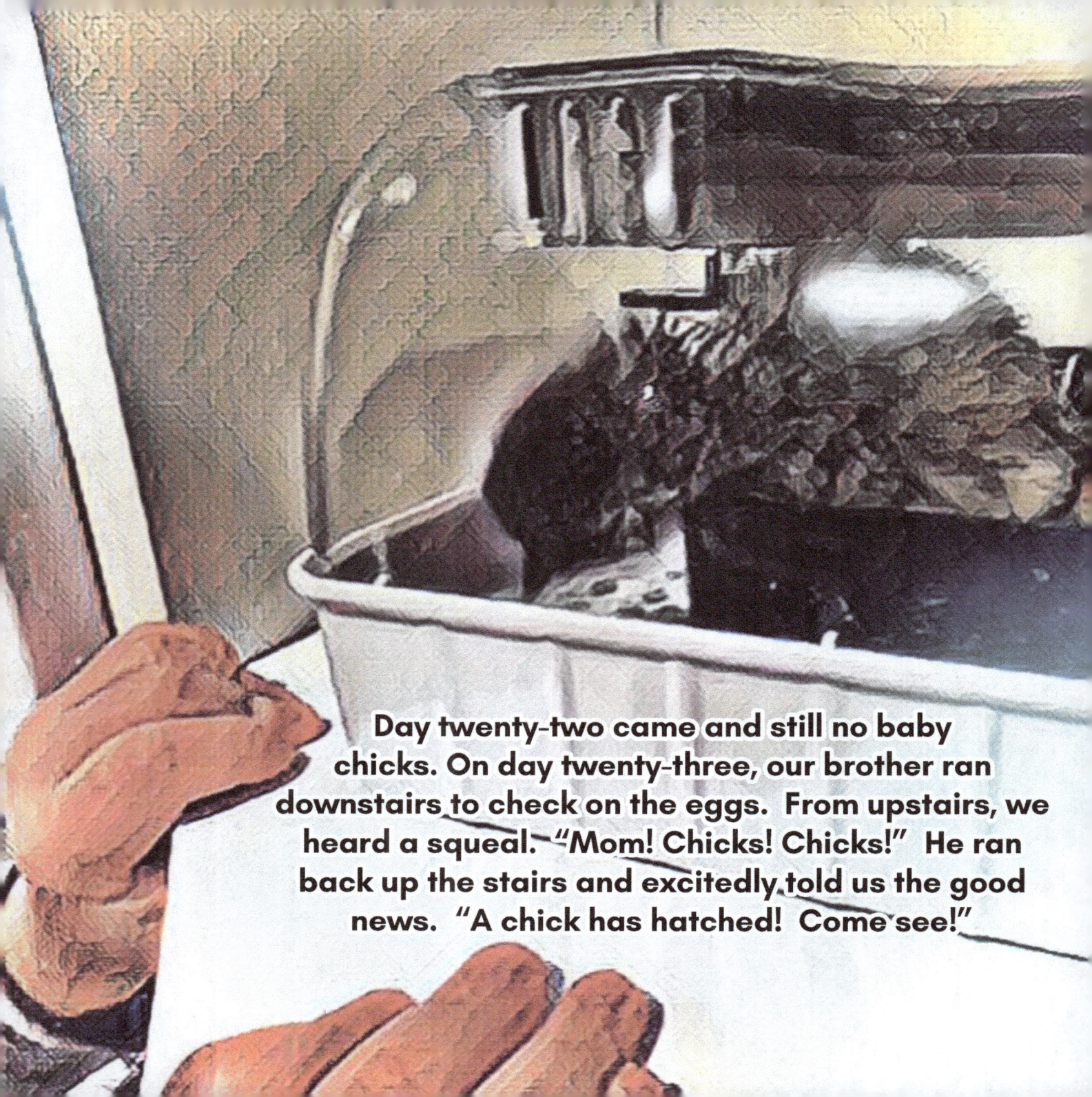

Day twenty-two came and still no baby chicks. On day twenty-three, our brother ran downstairs to check on the eggs. From upstairs, we heard a squeal. "Mom! Chicks! Chicks!" He ran back up the stairs and excitedly told us the good news. "A chick has hatched! Come see!"

The four of us peered into the incubator. In the corner was a black baby chick, sitting sleepily.

"The baby looks very tired, and she is very wet from the fluid in her egg. We must wait until her feathers dry off in the warm incubator. If we take her out too soon while her feathers are wet, she may get a chill and not survive."

We smiled at the baby chick from outside of the incubator. She would sleep and then wake up and walk on top of the other eggs.

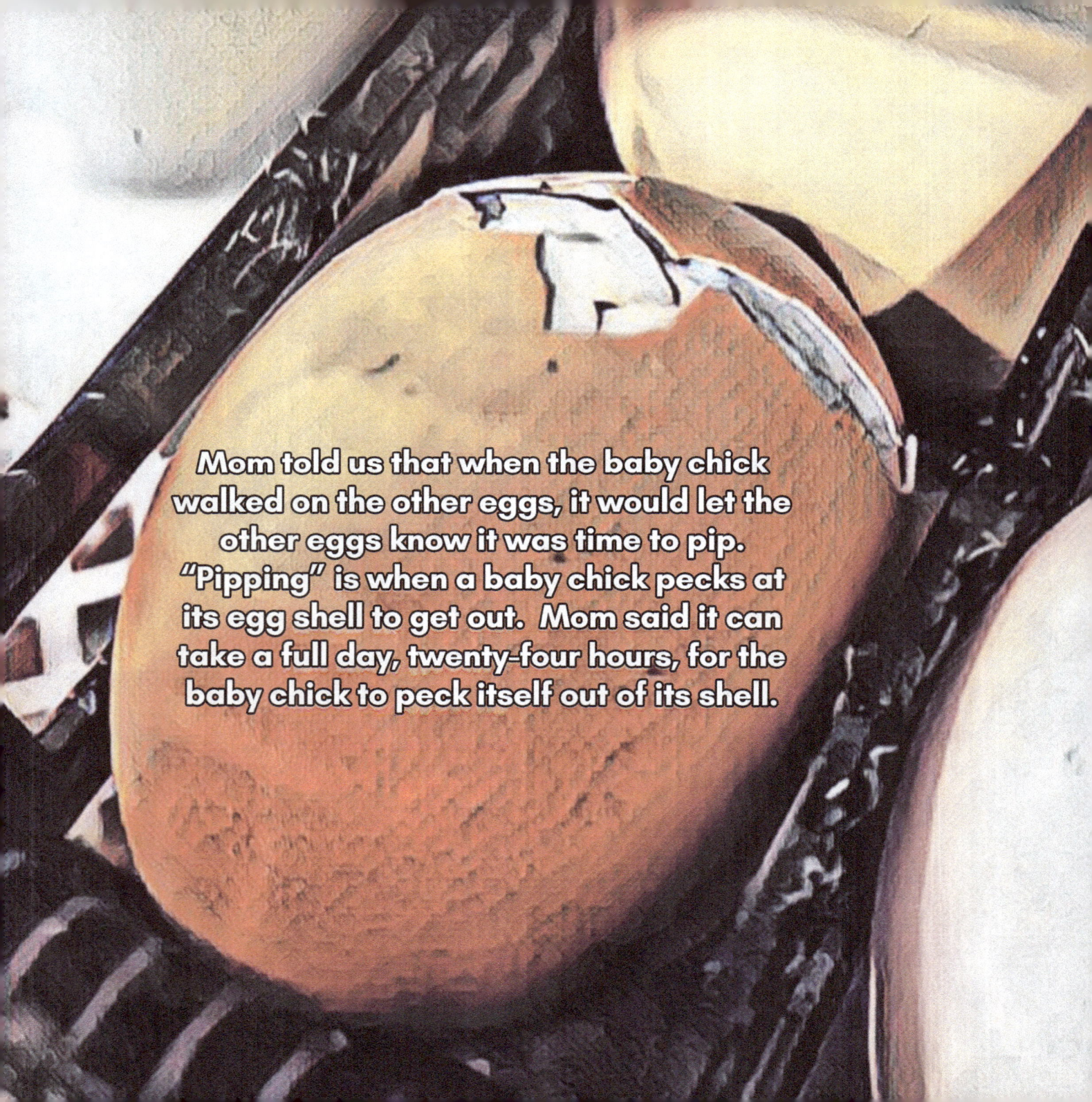

Mom told us that when the baby chick walked on the other eggs, it would let the other eggs know it was time to pip. "Pipping" is when a baby chick pecks at its egg shell to get out. Mom said it can take a full day, twenty-four hours, for the baby chick to peck itself out of its shell.

So, we waited and waited to see if more babies would hatch. Hours later, we noticed an egg was starting to crack!

The baby chick pecked and pecked until eventually we could see some of its little body.

The second baby chick finally sat outside of her eggshell and looked at the world around her. The two chicks wandered around the incubator together, and we waited patiently for them to dry off and fluff up.

The next day, three more babies were born! All together there were now five baby chicks – four black and grey chicks and one yellow chick with black speckles. Mom told us the dark chicks were Austrolorp chickens and the yellow one with black spots was a Crele Orpington chicken. They were all so cute!

Dad said we needed to make a home for the chicks to live in! He said a chicken house is called a brooder. We helped him get the brooder ready. We used a rabbit cage and put a layer of wood shavings on the bottom of the cage.

We then put a thermo-poultry brooder in the cage. This looks like a little orange table, and it emits heat. The chicks can huddle underneath it in the same way they would hide under their mama! Dad hung a heat lamp from the top of the cage too, just in case the chicks needed extra warmth.

We moved the brooder to our sister's room, and we visited the chicks many times a day! The chicks started to eat seeds and drink water. Mom said chickens are omnivores, meaning they will try to eat just about anything they can get their beaks on! They like to eat fruits, vegetables and grains.

We learned that Austrolorp chickens are from Australia and they lay light-brown eggs.

We also learned that Crele Orpington chickens are from Britain. They are a sweet and docile chicken, and they lay light-brown eggs too!

We learned to take care of the baby chicks and to hold them gently...

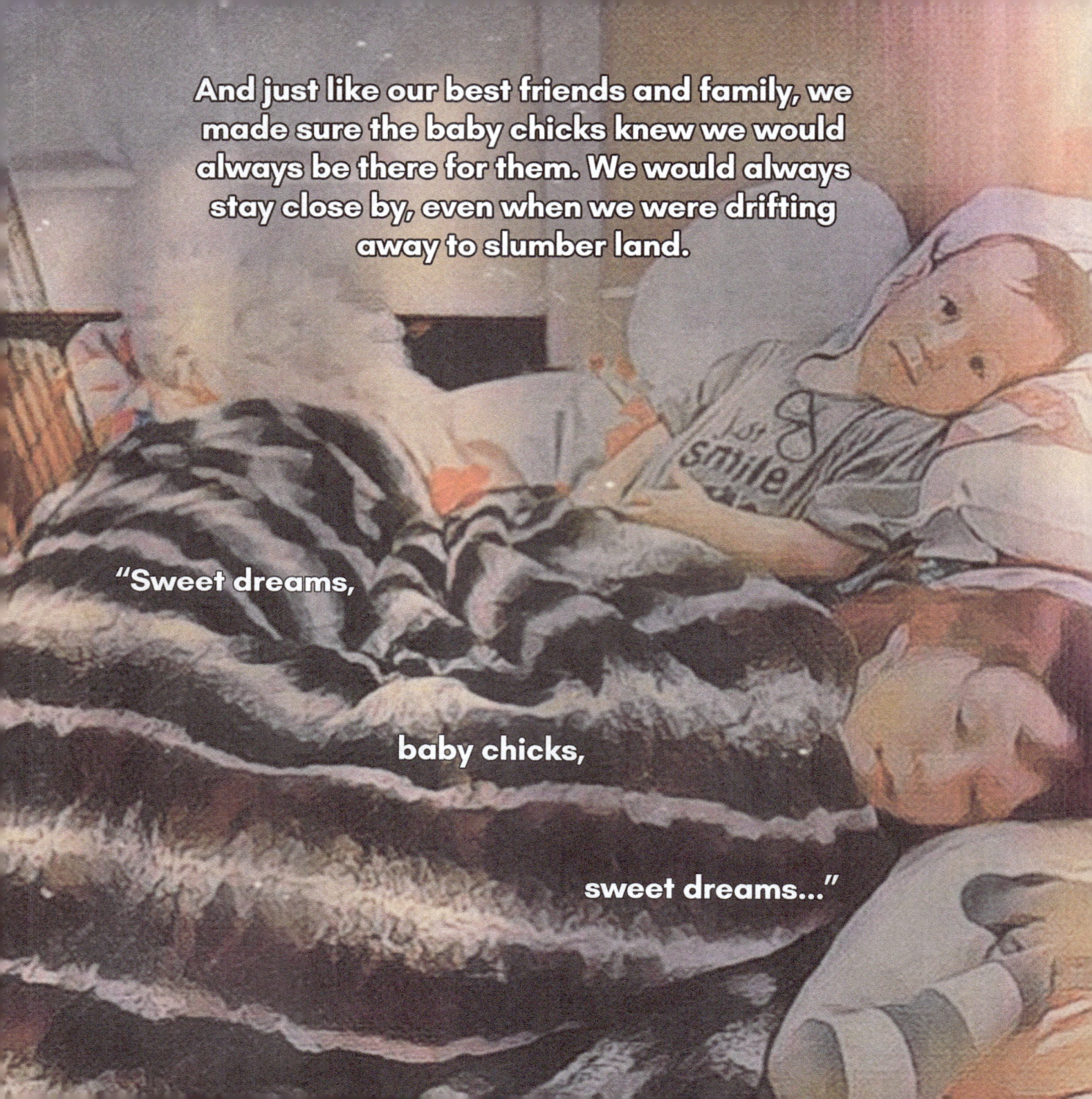

www.ingramcontent.com/pod-product-compliance
Lightning Source LLC
Chambersburg PA
CBHW081423080526
44589CB00016B/2645